This book belongs to

_____

This Book is about my

_____

This book was given to me by

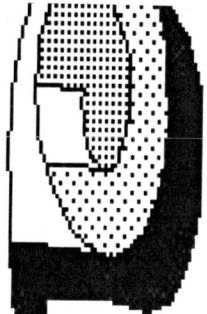

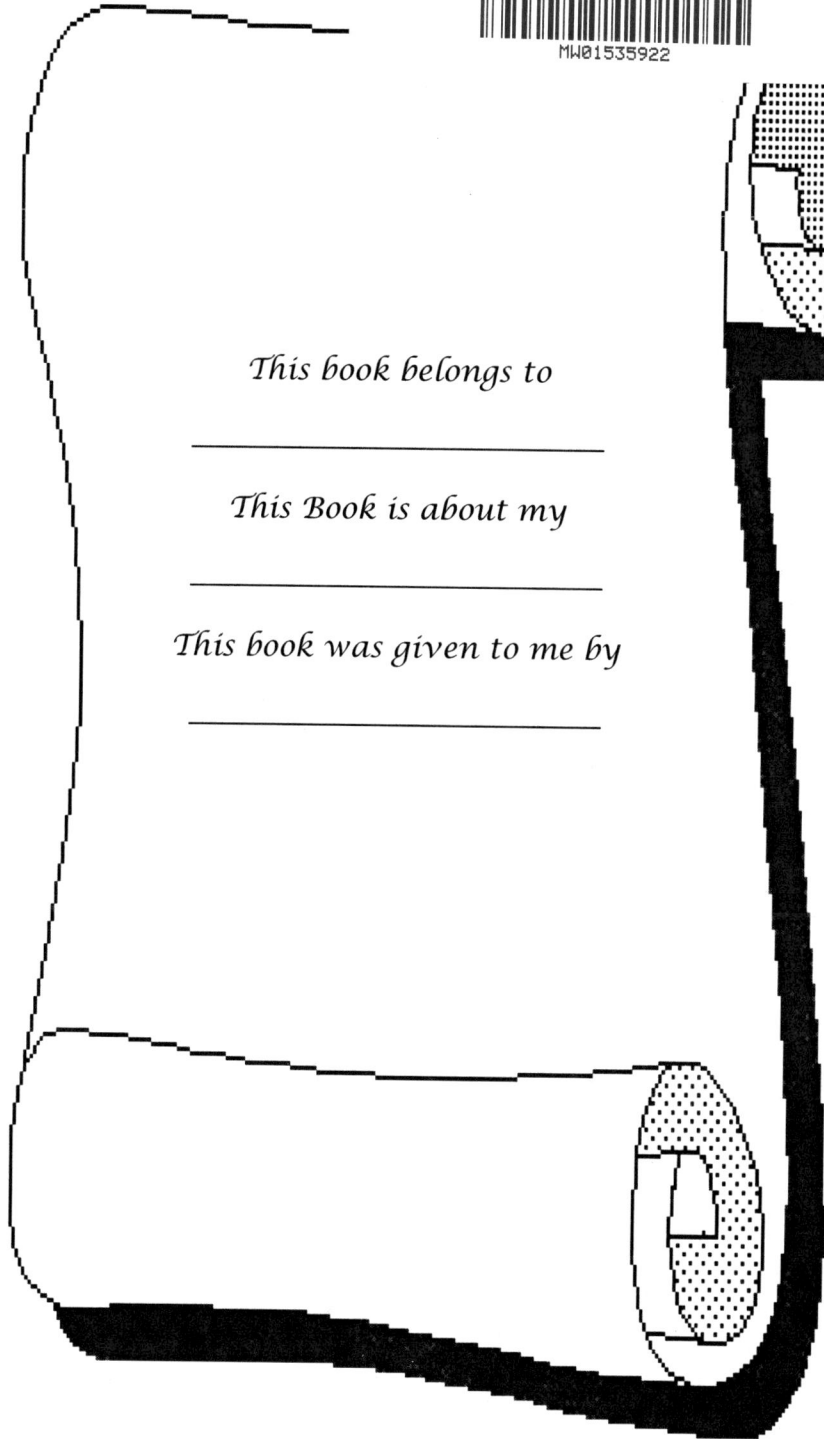

_____

A Time to Separate
A Time to Come Together

A Child's Workbook for Discovering and

Coping with the Hurt of Divorce, Managing

Anger, and Building a Better Tomorrow

Rabbi Rachmiel Tobesman

Copyright © 2009 by Rabbi Rachmiel Tobesman.

Library of Congress Control Number: 2008909600
ISBN: Hardcover   978-1-4363-8045-4
                Softcover   978-1-4363-8044-7

Project Shalom
PO Box 21549
Pikesville, Maryland 21282
(410) 358-0409

This book was printed in the United States of America.

To order additional copies of this book, contact:
Xlibris Corporation
1-888-795-4274
www.Xlibris.com
Orders@Xlibris.com
54748

Contents

In honor of my children

Benyomin, Shoshanah, and Yosef

What This Book Is about and
How to Use It

If you are reading this book, something sad probably happened in your family. Your parents have either separated or are getting a divorce. Things are probably real confusing, and you are angry and hurt.

This is your book. Most books you can only read; but you can write, draw, doodle, take notes, tape in pictures, and even fold the pages in this one. You can read, enjoy, learn, and share your thoughts in this book.

It is really hard to talk about what is happening in your life. You may even feel that no one can understand.

List as many words as you can that are used to mean *divorce*:

_____   _____

_____   _____

_____   _____

_____   _____

Look at all those words. Do they mean different things? Just like the words, you can have so many different feelings when confusing things happen. You might be sad, angry, mixed-up, or scared. At times, you may not feel anything at all. Your feelings might be going up and down like a roller coaster. One minute, you want to cry; and then, you just don't feel like crying. Some children feel unexpected things, like wanting to act silly or to laugh a lot. Sometimes, children feel guilty for things they did or for feelings they had about their parents.

What are some of the ways you have been feeling?

_____

_____

_____

_____

_____

The Torah is very important to the Jewish people. We believe there is a written Torah and an oral Torah. In other words, we have passed down our beliefs and traditions to our children. The Torah teaches us how to do many things to make the world a better place. Sometimes people become so lost in all that happens in their life. Torah helps us to find direction and solutions to our problems, fears, and concerns.

This book is to help you understand different things about separation and divorce in the Jewish community. There are stories, activities, and mysteries for you to explore. You can fill out the pages in the order they're written, or you can skip around. There may be some pages you don't want to do at all. That's okay. It's up to you.

There may be a lot of questions you have about what happened and about what's going to happen in the future. This book will help you to answer some of those questions and to encourage you to ask more questions. This is a book to help you in growing closer to your parents and family. As you fill in this book, you will be creating a special treasure that you can keep forever.

Weddings and Sheva Brachas

Rabbi Yitzchok Abarbanel once said that "love turns one person into two and two into one." As people fall in love, they plan a special day to get married. When the wedding day comes, they are filled with hope and joy. This is the happiest and holiest day of one's life. This day is so special for the *chasan* (groom) and *kallah* (bride) because on this day all their past mistakes are forgiven as they merge into a new life together.

הֲרֵי אַתְּ מְקֻדֶּשֶׁת לִי, בְּטַבַּעַת זוֹ, כְּדַת מֹשֶׁה וְיִשְׂרָאֵל

Haray aht mikudeshes li b'taba'as zu k'das moshe v'yisrael

Behold, you are consecrated to me with this ring
according to the Law of Moses and Israel.

With these traditional words, Jewish men and women have married one another for thousands of years. Each time these words are recited, a bride and groom have hopes and dreams for a lifetime of happiness together.

A new couple is brought together with *sheva brachas*, seven blessings. The seven blessings are repeated each day for seven days following the wedding so that their wedding and life together can be blessed.

There are many reasons why people get married. Write some reasons for marriage:

_____

_____

_____

_____

Some of these reasons may lead to the development of a strong and lasting marriage. But some may mean that the marriage will begin with problems and have a greater possibility of ending in divorce. Underline those reasons which you feel are healthy reasons to marry.

The Clever Wife

Long, long ago, there lived in an old town a happy couple named Avraham and Sarah. Although they loved one another very much, their happiness was not complete. They had been married for nearly ten years, but they had not been blessed with a child.

Sarah would often sit in her room and cry. She prayed every day to Hashem to grant her the blessing of having a son or a daughter. Avraham did his best to comfort her by telling her that Hashem heard her heartfelt prayer and would answer them at the right time.

At the same time, he felt very sad when he came home and thought of Sarah's pain. He would have given anything to have had a little son who might be taught the holy Torah which he loved so well.

The neighbors on their street were not too kind, and they hurt Sarah. This made her sadness more bitter. People often said, in Avraham's hearing, that children are a sign of Hashem's blessing. Was it not true that the house which lacked the merry laughter of little children was under a curse or spell? Did not the holy Torah teach that it was a mitzvah to marry and have children? Would it not be better, he argued with himself, to divorce his wife, if, after being married for ten years, she had no child? She might marry another man and have children and so find her happiness. All these thoughts flashed again and again through his mind.

At last when the anniversary of their tenth marriage day arrived, Avraham said to his wife, "Let us visit today our true friend and guide the holy rabbi to ask his advice on what we should do."

When they came before the holy rabbi, Avraham, with tears in his eyes, said, "Holy Rabbi! My dear wife has been faithful and loving to me during the past ten years. It has pleased Holy One, blessed be He to hold back from us the blessing of children. I fear this is on account of my many sins. It seems to me that our home from now on will not be as happy as it should be. my wife cries everyday, and I am sad because she is so unhappy. Is it not my duty to set her free?"

While Avraham was speaking, his wife wept. She knew that if he sent her away from his heart and home, her life would be really sad and lonely. Her deep sorrow touched the heart of her husband, who turned to her and cried, "My dear, sweet, beloved wife, do not cry and grieve, for we must submit to the will of the Holy One, blessed be He. Do not think that I am not often sad because we have no child to bring happiness to your long days. If I could only take away your sorrow and pain, I would most gladly do so. Listen, dearest! I faithfully promise to allow you to choose whatever you like best in our home, and you may take it with you to your father's house as a keepsake when you leave me for good. This will always be a visible token of the deep affection and true love which united us during the past ten years."

The holy rabbi watched Avraham and Sarah understanding their sorrow. He knew that Avraham had made up his mind to divorce his worthy wife. Nothing would make him change his mind. With a mystical wisdom, he spoke to them, "My dear children, I can only pity you, for I am deeply sorry to see how you are about to lose one another. Before you finally part, however, let me advise you to invite all your family and friends to a special seudah (meal) just as they gathered around you ten years ago at your marriage feast. Love united you and in love prepare to separate, if it must be." Avraham and Sarah promised to follow the advice of the rabbi, and they returned home.

Sarah at once sent to all their friends and provided a most generous meal with music and wine. Her husband sat beside her as usual, and she took care that his wineglass was constantly filled. Good cheer made everyone very happy, and Avraham was determined to spend a jolly evening for the last time in the company of his wife, whom he really loved.

Sarah had carefully prepared her plans. Her husband had spoken to each of his guests, and soon all the excitement made him very tired, and he fell deeply asleep. Without a moment's delay, Sarah called her servants. She told them to lift up the armchair in which her husband sat asleep and to carry it at once to her father's house in a neighboring street.

Meanwhile, Avraham, fast asleep, had been carried to his new quarters. He was put in a beautiful room, with Sarah at his side, waiting for him to awaken. At dawn he woke up. Looking around with great surprise, he exclaimed, "Where am I?"

Sarah took his hand, and stroking it gently, she said to him, My beloved! You are in my father's house."

"What am I doing here?" he cried.

"You are just waking up," she says. "You remember when we yesterday visited the holy rabbi, you faithfully promised me that I might choose anything I liked best in our home and take it with me when I left your roof. Last night I left your house, and I took you with me as there was nothing in your home or, for the matter of that, in all the world so precious to me as your dear self. You were the choicest possession in our old home, and you are mine now and forever. You have, by your promise to me, given yourself over to me. Divorce or no divorce, you are my property, for I know very well you always keep your promise."

Avraham saw the humor of the situation in which he found himself and laughed again and again at the wisdom and love of his clever wife. "Well done," he exclaimed, "we are now agreed that the question of divorce is solved. Once again are we united and this time forever. Nothing shall part us as long as we live."

Like all good people, they lived a very happy life. In time a son was born and later on a daughter was given to them, and they all rejoiced in one another's happiness.

Based on Song of Songs Rabbah 1:4

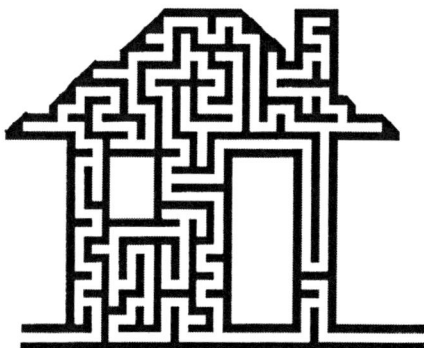

Sarah's House

```
                        A
      W   W   E       K   P   V
      E   V   Z     G   G   D   H   R
      D   Y   V   I   C   J   I   D   U   A
      D   Y   R   S   C   K   V   B   B   S   H
      I   Y   M   L   H   A   O   M   A   G   B   A
      N   K   H   E   I   L   R   H   S   R   U   A   M
    Y   G   A   D   E   L   L   C   H   H   O   T   W   N   N
  K   L   R   I   Y   P   D   A   E   Y   H   O   O   E   M   D   T
  O   A   R   P   C   I   R   H   U   A   Z   M   R   L   A   F   E
  S   B   P   D   H   B   E   O   D   W   C   T   A   G   R   F   N
  O   A   G   H   A   M   N   U   B           H   K   I   F   Y
  H   R   M   V   S   L   E   G   E           E   L   C   Q   E
  H   W   E   I   A   S   O   W   X           L   Y   S   B   A
  R   H   A   T   N   Q   Z   V   Q           W   I   F   E   R
  S   O   L   R   A   B   B   I   E           G   H   Q   O   S
  B   L   E   S   S   I   N   G   V           Z   W   F   W   J
```

Avraham	Happy	Sarah
Blessing	Husband	Seudah
Bride	Kallah	Sheva Brachas
Chasan	Life	Sleep
Children	Love	Ten Years
Divorce	Meal	Torah
Groom	Rabbi	Wedding
		Wife

The Jewish View of Divorce

"This shall be for you from me a bill of dismissal, a letter of release, and a document of freedom, in accordance with the laws of Moses and Israel."

The hopes and dreams of some couples are not reached. Not all marriages last a lifetime. Some end in divorce. Divorce means the legal ending of a marriage. The words above are from a Jewish divorce document.

The Hebrew word for betrothal is kiddushin (קִדּוּשִׁין) which means sanctification or holiness is very similar to the word *kiddush* (קִידּוּשׁ) which means "to make holy." Just from the word *kiddushin,* we can begin to understand Judaism's attitude about marriage.

Rabbis through our long history have spoken out against divorce:

Many embark on marriage, most succeed, and some come to grief (Numbers Rabbah).

If a man divorces his first wife, very altar weeps (Gittin 90b).

A woman may not be divorced except by her own consent (Decree of Rabbeinu Gershom c. 1000 CE).

A man without a wife lives without good, without help, without joy, without blessing and with out forgiveness (Koheles Rabbah 9:7).

A married man receives a double blessing from God: one for himself, and one for his wife (Zohar I, 233b).

If it will says, "My husband is unpleasant to me, I cannot live with him," the court makes the husband to divorce her, because the wife is not a captive (Maimonides [Rambam], Yad Ishut 14.8).

Why do you think marriage is something holy in the Jewish religion?

_____

_____

_____

_____

Even though marriage is holy, Jewish tradition has always recognized that some circumstances justify ending a marriage. In fact, the possibility for divorce was provided for even in the marriage contract.

Jewish Customs and Traditions

The traditional Jewish marriage contract is called a ketubah (כתובה). It is often very artistic and beautiful yet always very practical. The ketubah assures the bride that the husband will be loving toward her and provide for her. It also lists the financial support she will receive in case the husband divorces her.

A Jewish divorce paper is called a Get (גט), meaning document. The need for such a document is mentioned in the Torah in Deuteronomy 24:1-4.

Find this section in your Chumash or Bible.
What does it say? (Rewrite it in your own words.)

_____

_____

_____

_____

What do you think the rabbis are saying about divorce? _____

_____

_____

_____

This is what a Get says:

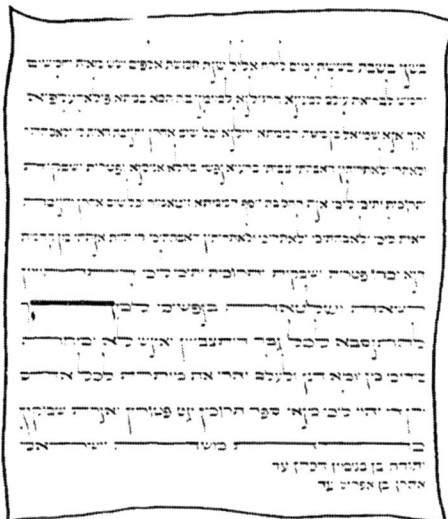

On the _____ day of the week, the _____ day of the _____ month of _____ in the year _____ from the creation of the world according to the calendar reckoning we are accustomed to count here, in the city (which is also known as _____), which is located on the river _____ (and on the river _____) and situated near wells of water, _____ also known as _____), the son of _____ (also known as _____), who today am present in the city _____ (which is also known as _____), which is located on the river _____ (and on the river _____), and situated near wells of water, do willingly consent, being under no restraint, to release, to set free, and put aside you, my wife, _____ (also known as _____), daughter of (also known as _____), who is today in the city of _____ (which is also known as _____), which is located on the _____ river (and on the river _____), and situated near wells of water, who has been my wife from before. Thus I do set free, release you, and put you aside, in order that you may have permission and the authority over yourself to go and marry any man you may desire. No person may hinder you from this day onward, and you are permitted to every man. This shall be for you from me a bill of dismissal, a letter of release, and a document of freedom, in accordance with the laws of Moses and Israel.

_____ the son of _____ witness

_____ the son of _____ witness

Here are the necessary procedures for writing and giving a legal Get:

1. Must be twelve lines long. Must be written in Aramaic by a sofer, meaning scribe, who knows the correct wording and form.

2. Must be written on heavy white paper. Special ink and a pen made of goose quill or wood are used to write the text.

3. Two competent Jewish men must witness the writing of the Get and must read the Get before they sign it.

4. The names of the parties and their places of residence must be spelled absolutely correctly. This is in order that the Get cannot be used by someone else and so that the parties involved can be positively identified.

5. The husband must be the active agent. He must cause the document to be written because it is he who divorces the wife. He must do so of his own free will.

6. The husband asks the witnesses to witness the giving of the Get.

7. The Get must be hand delivered to the woman or her agent by the husband or his agent. As he hands the Get to his wife, he recites the following words in Hebrew, "This is your Get. Receive this Get. And you are divorced with this Get from me from now on. And you are free to marry any man."

8. The wife must remove all jewelry from her hands. She holds her hands palms up to receive the Get from her husband. She folds her hands over the Get, raises it in both hands, places it under her left arm next to her heart, then walks with the document about twelve feet in order to show that it is her property. Then she hands it to the rabbi.

9. The rabbi takes the Get from her. He opens it, and he and the witnesses read it again. The rabbi then slices it crosswise with a knife so that it cannot be used again. The Get is filed, and the couple receives a written statement (petur), stating that they received a Jewish divorce.

Jewish Views and Torah

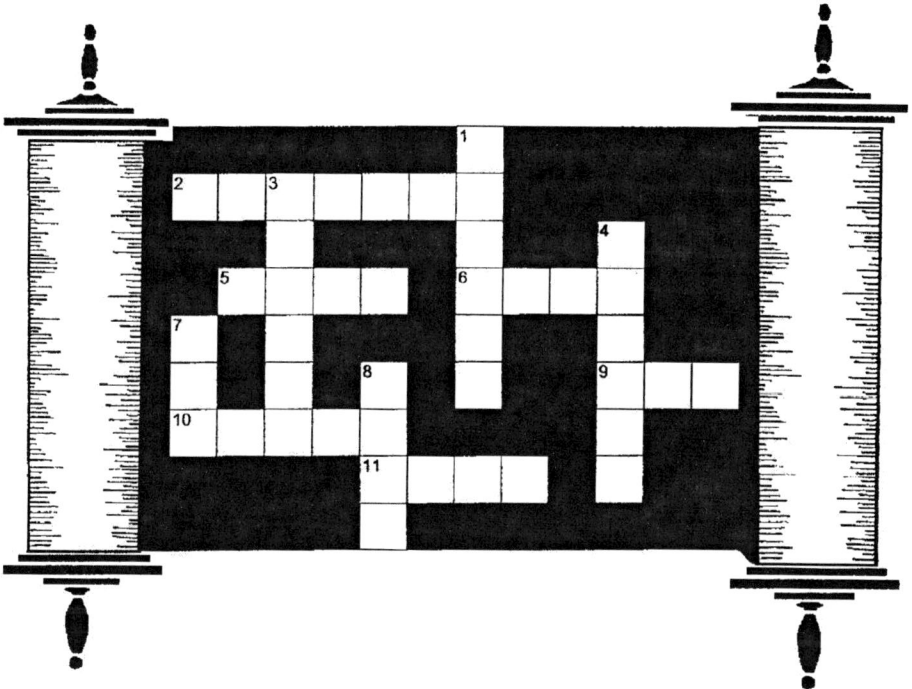

Across

2. Jewish Marriage Contract
5. Garden of _____
6. Rachel's Sister
9. Used to write with
10. Five Books of Moses
11. Pirke _____

Down

1. Peace
2. Prayerbook
4. Wedding canopy
6. Garden of _____
7. Jewish Divorce
8. Life

WORD BANK: Avos, chai, chupah, Eden, get, kesubah, Leah, pen, shalom, siddur, Torah

When Parents Argue

Just because your mother and father argue doesn't mean they are splitting up. But if you think they are splitting up, remember these important things:

- It's not your fault! Never. Nothing you have done has made your parents split up. Your parents are still your mother and your father and always will be. They are having problems with each other, not you.

- Your mother and father still love and care about you even if they don't always behave as if they do.

- You are still you, whatever happens, and you are very special.

Rabbi Meir Settles an Argument between Husband and Wife

Rabbi Meir used to give regular Torah lessons in the synagogue every Sabbath eve. A certain woman of that town made it a habit to listen to his weekly Torah lessons. On one occasion when he extended it to a late hour, she waited and did not leave until he finished.

When she came to her home, she found that the lamp was out. Her husband asked her, "Where have you been until now?"

She told him, "I have been listening to a Torah lesson."

Now the husband was not very nice and did not believe her. So he said to her, "I swear that you are not to enter my house again until you spit in the rabbi's face."

She left the house and stayed away one week, a second, and a third. Finally the neighbors asked her, "Are you still angry with each other? Let us go with you to the rabbi." When Rabbi Meir saw them, he knew the reason for their coming by means of the Holy Spirit. And so, pretending to be suffering from pain in the eyes, he asked, "Is there among you a woman skilled in whispering a charm for eye pain?" Her neighbors said to her, "Go, whisper in his ear and spit lightly in his eyes, and you will be able to live with your husband again." So she came forward. However, when she sat down before Rabbi Meir, she was so overawed by his presence that she confessed, "My master, I do not know how to whisper a charm for eye pain."

But he said to her, "Nevertheless, spit in my face seven times, and I will be healed."

She did so, whereupon he said, "Go and tell your husband, 'You bade me do it only once. I spat seven times!'"

His students said to him, "Master! Is the Torah to be treated with such contempt? If you had only mentioned it to us, would we not have brought that man and flogged him at the post until he consented to be reconciled with his wife?"

Rabbi Meir replied, "The dignity of Meir ought not to be greater than that of his Maker. If scripture enjoins that G-d's holy name, which is inscribed in sanctity, may be wiped out in water in order to bring about peace between a man and his wife, all the more so may Meir's dignity be disregarded" (P. Sot 1:4, 16d; Num. R. 9:20; Deut. R. 5:15; Lev. R. 9:9.).

Color the synagogue

15

Rabbi Meir Crossword Puzzle

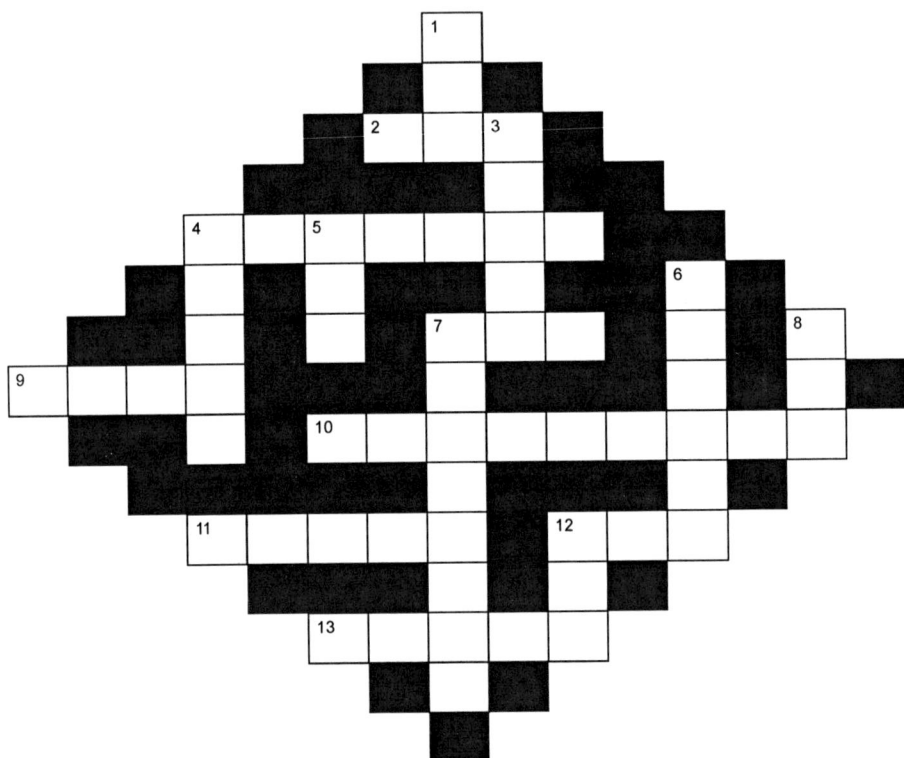

Across

2. Opposite of old
4. The seventh day
7. Weep
9. Opposite of husband
10. Agreed
11. Opposite of war
12. Little boy
13. Erased

Down

1. _____, two, three
3. H2O
4. 5,6, _____,8,9 . . .
5. Where someone sleeps
6. Hear
7. Disrespect
8. From the past
12. Gloomy

Talking to Your Parents
about the Divorce

Sometimes it's hard to tell your parents how you feel. You may feel embarrassed, angry, confused, afraid, or even a little guilty, thinking that you may have caused your parents to separate or divorce. Guess what? *You didn't.*

Don't keep things to yourself. Your feelings and thoughts are important. It is always best to tell your parents how you feel. They may not be aware that you feel bad about the divorce. They may want to talk to you about it too. Here are some ideas that might help:

- You could write them a letter and tell them how you feel.
- You could draw them a picture to tell them how you feel.
- You could ask them to set aside a certain time so that you can talk about the separation and divorce with them.

You will feel better after you talk to them. Don't expect that this will change the situation. It might help with certain parts of it. It will also help you feel better, and it may help your parents to understand you better.

Divorce Isn't So Scary Word Search

```
              J   F                   A   S
          Q   U   R   V           T   A   L   K
      W   B   D   I   V   O   R   C   E   F   G
  D   J   C   G   E   C   H   I   L   D   R   E   N
L O V   E   E   N   H   E   F   E   E   L   T   D   J
C O U   R   T   D   K   L   E   T   T   E   R   R   L
R A B   B   I   Z   P   P   A   F   E   W   I   A   X
  V   I   S   I   T   A   C   S   A   A   R   A   W
    N   B   C   A   R   E   K   T   C   I   L
    L   A   W   Y   E   R   S   H   H   T   I
        E   R   T   N   Y   U   E   E   E
            M   O   T   H   E   R   R
                E   S   E   E   K
                P   R   O
                O
```

Ask	Draw	Hero	Mother	Teacher
Care	Father	Judge	Parents	Trial
Children	Feel	Lawyers	Rabbi	Visit
Court	Friend	Letter	Seek	Write
Divorce	Help	Love	Talk	

Anger, Divorce, and Children

Just because your mother and father argue doesn't mean they are splitting up or getting a divorce. Being angry is part of life.

You probably don't need to explain what it means to be angry. You have most likely been angry at one time.

Can you remember a time when you were angry? _____

_____

How did you feel? _____

_____

It just happens that sometimes you mother and father get angry too. You may really be surprised to learn that the Torah talks about anger.

The Torah tells us that G-d gets angry too. When Moses was on the top of Mount Sinai, the children of Israel forgot part of the Ten Commandments and built a golden calf, an idol. G-d became so angry He said, "I have seen this people, and, behold, it is a stiff-necked people. Now let me alone, that my anger may burn hot against them, and that I may consume them"(Exodus 32:9-10).

Moses knew how angry G-d was and wanted to calm Him down and said, "Lord, why does your anger burn hot against your people, whom you have brought out of the land of Egypt with great power, and with a mighty hand" (Exodus 32:11).

In time, G-d calmed down, and Moses says, "Adonai, Adonai is a G-d, who is merciful and gracious, slow to anger, full of goodness and truth. Extending mercy to for thousands, forgiving iniquity and transgression and sin" (Exodus 34:6-7).

What are some things that G-d may get angry about? _____

_____

_____

_____

How did Moses help G-d calm down? _____

_____

_____

_____

Sometimes when people are angry, they say terrible and hurtful things they might not mean to say. Afterward, they are sad and ashamed at what was said and don't know how to make up and say they are sorry.

Nurturing Ways to Handle Your Anger

While hurt is something you feel inside and you may not want to tell anyone about, anger, on the other hand, is your hurt turned toward others. It is not wrong to feel angry. If someone hurts you a lot and does not seem to want to be fair toward you, it is only natural that you get upset and angry toward that person.

Feeling anger and expressing anger are healthy for everyone. There is nothing wrong with the feeling of anger. What gets a lot of people in trouble is how they express their anger. Taking anger out on yourself, on someone else, or on objects is never okay. Hitting, yelling, and belittling and doing things that injure yourself or harm the environment are not appropriate ways of expressing anger.

Are you angry or upset with someone or something that happened?

_____

_____

_____

One thing that happened or person that I am angry with is _____

_____

Why are you angry at this thing that happened or person? _____

_____

_____

_____

When I am angry, I am most likely to _____

_____

_____

When this happens, I feel, and those around me feel

_____

_____

There are rules for almost everything. Three rules for expressing anger in a way that is okay are the following:

Never do anything to hurt yourself, someone else, or your surroundings.

Here are some ways of expressing anger without hurting yourself, someone else, or anything around you:

Angry Letter

Write a short letter to each person you are angry with. Tell them that you are angry with them for what they did or failed to do. Put each letter in its own envelope, and place it where you can easily see it. When you feel the anger again, open it up and add how you are feeling to the end of it. Keep the letter for as long as you feel better when you look at it. After you no longer have the need to look at the letter, get rid of it. Make it a meaningful occasion. *Whatever you do, don't mail the letter to the person. This is your private letter.*

Monster Masks

Anger can be scary and sometimes bigger than we can handle, especially when those around us seem to be angry a lot. Well, monsters are scary sometimes too. Right?

___

Let's see if we can make a little less scary; ask your mother of father to help you get together these stuff: paper bag, scissors, some magic markers, crayons, macaroni, beans, rice, cotton, and glue

What you are going to do is make a monster mask. What is a monster?

_____

Are monsters good or bad? _____

What does a monster look like? _____

_____

Take you paper bag and have your mother or father cut openings in the brown paper bag for your eyes. Now decorate the monster mask any way you want.

How do monsters act? Take your monster mask and have a good time playing. Remember while you are playing to have fun.

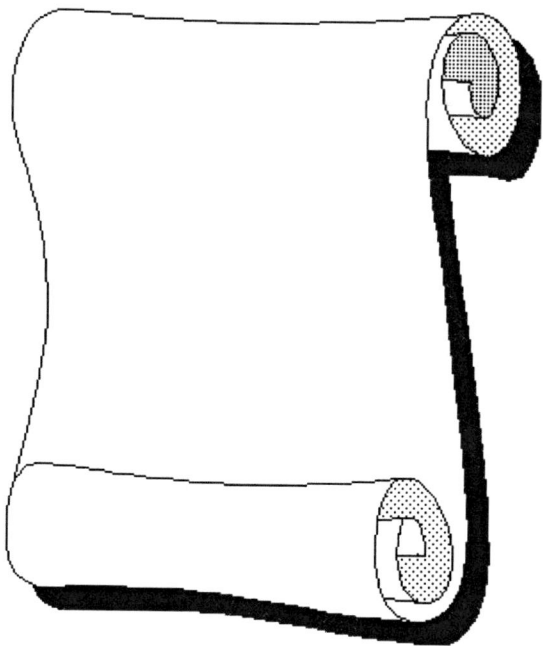

Angry Bread

Have you ever gotten so angry that you just want to hit someone or something? Well, here is a really neat way of doing just that and having some real good fun. And you know what else? Your parents might have some fun doing this with you.

First, you have to get all the baking stuff together. You're going to need a bit of help from your mother or father. Gather together the following:

4 Cups	All Purpose Flour (Bread flour works best)
2 Tablespoons	Sugar
1Package	Yeast
1 Cup	Warm water or milk
1 Teaspoon	Salt
4 Tablespoons	Margarine or oil
1 Large	Egg (beaten)

Egg Wash (beat 1 egg with 1 tablespoon of water)

Now here are the directions. Follow them carefully:

1. Dissolve the sugar in 1/4 cup of warm milk or water in a cup or small bowl. Ad yeast and let sit until foamy.

2. Combine foamy yeast with milk or water.

3. Gradually beat in the milk or water into 1 1/4 cups of the flour to make a smooth batter.

   This is a good time to talk about what's bothering you.

4. Slowly add the oil or margarine, the egg, the salt, and the remaining flour and the salt.

24

5.   Mix well to a fairly soft dough that leaves the sides of the bowl clean.

6.   Knead for 10 minutes.

Beating up the dough helps get some of the anger out.

7.   Let rise approximately 1 hour or until double in size.

Talk some more, discuss choices, or do something fun together.

8.   Knock back the risen dough and then knead again for 3 to 5 minutes.

Still angry? Take it out on the dough.

9.   Separate into two portions and place in loaf pans. Let dough rise 45 minutes or until doubled.

10. Brush the loaves with the egg wash.

11. Bake in preheated oven 350° for 35 to 45 minutes. The crust will be golden brown, and the bread will sound hollow when tapped. Cool about 15 minutes on a wire rack.

*Now the best part, slice some bread and eat it
with some butter or jam or just plain.*

It's always better to eat the anger instead of the anger eating you.

If you are adventurous, you may want to try some of these ideas:

Knot Rolls

Roll out dough to strands about 4-6 inches long. Take the two ends of the strand and loop them to form a knot. Repeat with the remaining dough.

Coils

Roll out 2 oz. dough to a strand about 4-6 inches long. Coil up the dough from one end. Repeat with the remaining dough.

Cloverleaf Rolls

Shape into smooth small balls. Arrange in clusters of three on a greased baking sheet, making sure that the three pieces of dough touch each other. Repeat with the remaining dough.

After shaping the rolls, place them on greased baking sheets, spacing them well apart. Let the dough rise until double in size. Brush with egg wash and sprinkle with poppy or sesame seeds or leave plain. Bake the rolls for 25-30 minutes until golden brown and they sound hollow when tapped underneath. Cool on a wire rack.

If You Think Your Parents
Are Splitting Up

Remember these important things:

- ❖ It's not your fault!
- ❖ Nothing you have done has made your parents split up.
- ❖ Your parents are still your mother and your father and always will be.
- ❖ They are having problems with each other, not you.
- ❖ Your mother and father still love and care about you very much even if they don't always act as if they do.

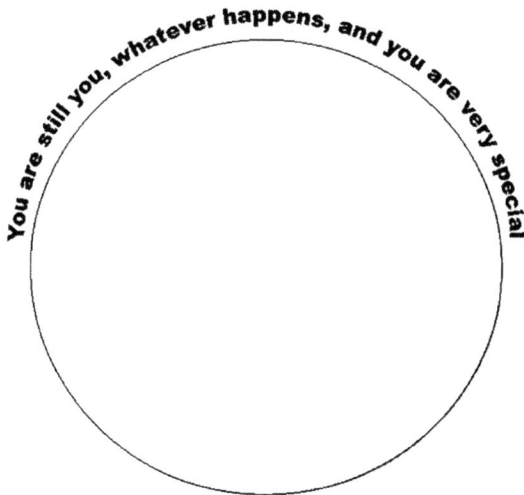

You are still you, whatever happens, and you are very special

Draw a picture of yourself in the circle

Lashon haRa—Hurtful Language

Lashon haRa is Hebrew for "an evil tongue." It teaches that some of the words we speak with our tongues can do harm.

Rabban Shimon ben Gamaliel said to his servant, Tabbai, "Go to the market and buy me some good food." The servant went and brought back a tongue.

He told him, "Go out and bring me some bad food from the market." The servant went and brought back a tongue.

The rabbi said to him, "Why is it that when I said good food you bought me at tongue, and when I said bad food you also bought me a *tongue*?"

The servant replied, "It is source of good and evil. When *it is good, there is* nothing *better.* When it is evil, there is nothing worse." (Leviticuṣ Rabbah 33:1)

Sometimes our tongues can speak words that help people. Some of our words can feel like hugs or handshakes. Sometimes words can make us feel better. We can speak words that help others. We can speak words that do good.

Hurting with words is worse than hurting with swords because while swords do their damage from nearby, words can wound at a great distance (Jerusalem Talmud Peah 1:1).

Hurting with words is worse than hitting at person. Hitting will affect the body, but words go much deeper. Bruises from at hit heal eventually. Wounds from words may never be healed (Vilna Gaon).

To everything there is a season, and a time to every purpose under the heaven . . . A time to keep silence and a time to speak (Ecclesiastes 3:1, 7).

And you shall teach them diligently unto your children, and shall talk of them when you sit in your house, and when you walk by the way, and when you lie down and when you rise up (Deuteronomy 6:7).

What Do You Think?

What are some words that have hurt you? _____

_____

_____

_____

_____

What are some words that have healed you? _____

_____

_____

_____

_____

What words should we teach our children? _____

_____

_____

_____

_____

When is it wise to be silent? _____

_____

_____

_____

_____

When should one speak? _____

_____

_____

_____

_____

Before Speaking, Weigh Your Words (Derech Eretz 1:30)

Lamed Puzzle

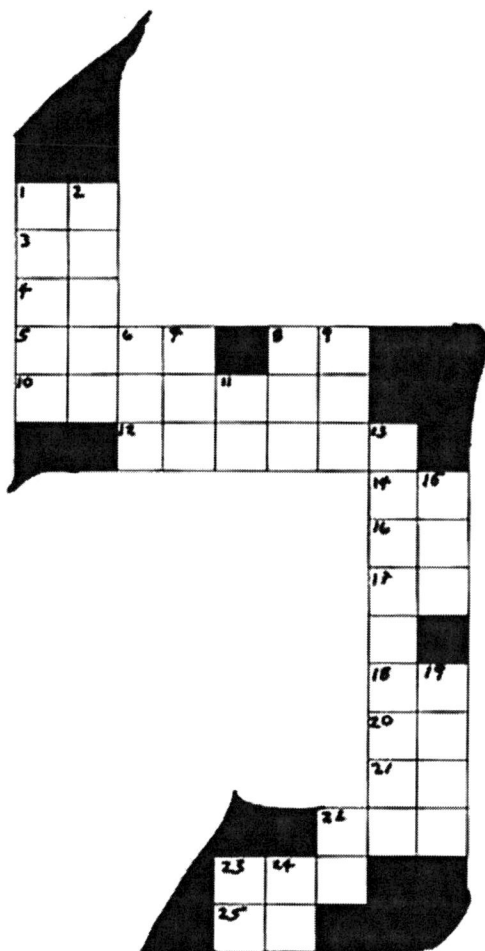

Across
1. No in Hebrew
2. Nickname for Albert
3. Third note of the scale
4. Always
8. Height abbrev.
10. Samson's betrayer
12. Reflections in a mirror
14. Immediately, _____ once
16. Opposite of *yes*
18. Doctor abbrev.
20. Receiving Office abbrev.
21. Exists
22. First number
23. *From* in Hebrew
25. Old Testament abbrev.

Down
1. Hebrew letter in puzzle
2. _____ branch
6. High priest and judge who trained Samuel
7. Edge
8. Old witch
9. Definite article
11. Louisiana abbrev.
13. Highest court of Jewish law
15. Digit on foot
19. _____ of Sharon
22. Atop
23. Home state of President Truman abbrev.
24. Italy abbrev.

The Magic Glasses

nce upon a time in a kingdom far away, a prince was born to a king and queen. The palace was filled with love for the prince. One day the clouds grew dark, and a terrible war with bitter fighting came to the kingdom. The little prince saw the war breaking out in first one place and then the other so that often he couldn't even tell which side was which. Finally, he became so sad, confused, and afraid that he stopped talking and sharing and was always by himself in order to make it through each day.

The queen told the little prince that if he would only wear magic glasses she had, he would feel better; she put the magic glasses on him, letting him know that his eyes needed to be protected from the war and demanding that he wear them at all times. However, when the prince went around to the king, the king would throw away those glasses, saying that his glasses could protect the prince, not the queen's glasses, and that the powerful glasses' strength were what the boy should wear in order to see better and get rid of his sadness. The poor prince seemed always to be changing glasses—first wearing those from the king and then having to change into the queen's glasses when she was around. The fighting over the glasses went on all the time, and to tell the truth, the prince found it very difficult to see through either pair of glasses. Whenever he had them on and looked around, the world looked dark and gloomy—all black and red. Sometimes the prince wore both sets of glasses at once, and this really caused the world to appear scary and strange.

Because the little prince spent so much time changing from one pair of glasses to another and trying to remember which pair he should be wearing, he had trouble learning, growing, and making friends. He became lonelier and even more withdrawn, and deep within him was a longing that he couldn't explain. One day he was in the palace garden trying to look at the trees and flowers. As usual, he was having trouble seeing where he was going because of the glasses; on this particular day, he had both sets of glasses on. Suddenly he heard a tiny giggle.

As he tried to locate the sound, the giggle turned into a louder laugh, but because of the glasses, the poor prince could not see where it was coming from. Not far from his foot was a another boy holding his stomach in laughter as seeing this strange sight of a prince wearing two sets of thick, cloudy glasses. The more the boy giggled, the angrier the prince became.

"Who's that laughing at me?" he cried.

"It's me!" replied a voice near the ground.

"Where are you? Show yourself this very minute!" commanded the prince, trying to sound as royal as possible.

"I'm right here in front of you," said the boy. "If you would only take off those glasses, you could easily see me!"

"But I can't!" said the prince sadly. "I have to wear at least one pair all the time, and sometimes two! The king and queen have said so!"

"What is it like when you look through them?" asked the boy.

"Well, it doesn't look good," replied the prince. "It looks ugly and sad and angry."

"The world is really not like that," said the boy, who was no longer laughing. "It's time you realized you have a choice. You may keep wearing the glasses, or you may take them off. Why don't you try taking them off and looking at the world as others see it? Then you can decide whether you want to put them back on again or not."

The prince was a little afraid to take off the glasses, recalling his parents demanding over and over that he wear them because they said so. But he really wanted to be able to see where he was headed too, so he removed the glasses. Turning his head from side to side, he beheld the beauty of the garden with its rainbow of colors and was filled with joy. Looking ahead, he saw the smiling face the boy.

"The choice is yours now," said the boy. "You really don't need glasses at all. Your eyes are the best of anyone around, and it would seem silly to wear glasses that make the world look different than it really is."

Nobody had ever talked to the little prince in that way before, and he thought about what the boy had said. Then he knew: he *did* have a choice! He wanted from that day forward to see the world *without* those glasses! The prince and his new friend talked and talked after that about life and seeing and the beauty that was all around.

The king and queen, of course, very hopping mad that the boy no longer wore their glasses, demanded that he put them on again at once. But the prince refused; he could see in a different way now and said that his vision was perfectly fine. He told them that he was able to look at the war and confusion in the kingdom in a new way which wasn't so scary, and he enjoyed seeing all the colors and the beauty around him. The boy helped the prince realize that his world was not so full of conflict and doubt as he had feared before, that he was free to make new friends and to learn and to grow as he was intended to do. When the prince grew to be a man and became king himself, he ruled the kingdom in a very different way than his parents had.

And he made sure that he never wore glasses that he didn't need.

Let's Make a Bookmark

Draw pictures on the bookmark that will have a special meaning for others. Use pictures and words. Color the bookmark to make them even more special!

The Magic Glasses Puzzle

```
    R Z Z A O J              A V H X G K
  H T E F Z Z T G          X W F Z A F N N
H P T R M L C E R U      M O I H R I P E I S
G L A S S E S V W E      C N Z O G M E P A K
F I T R T T M O L R W L D Y Y H D U D S Y J
D M E O E S B B E D O O F A T L Q D A R K G
G A R D E N U T E U      L T S T E F G L A D
Z P O Y I O T V D R      Y F R I E N D B U O
  N E A R E O S V          M D E A R O V U
    R T B L W R              T U E Y P L
```

There are thirty-eight words hidden in the magic glasses. Can you find them?

Afraid	Find	Laugh	Remember
Angry	Flower	Lonely	Royal
Better	Friend	Love	Sad
Boy	Garden	Parents	Safe
Clouds	Glad	Pretty	Tree
Dark	Glasses	Protect	Trouble
Eyes	Happy	Queen	
Fight	King	Rainbow	

But I Feel Like My Whole World Just Fell Apart!

If your parents are separated or if your family is going through a divorce, there are a few important things about feelings you need to remember. First of all, it's normal to feel lots of different things, including anger, fear, and sadness.

Second, even though it may seem as if your whole world just fell apart, with time, things will be better again. Your life might be a little different, but the pieces will come back together again—maybe even sooner than you think.

In the mean time, there are ways you can deal with the feelings you have. If you are really angry, remember the three rules for expressing anger in a way that is okay. *Never do anything to hurt yourself, someone else, or your surroundings.*

Telling someone how you feel can also help. If you feel really angry, say so. Talking is much better than keeping your feelings to yourself or acting all grouchy and irritable.

Sometimes just talking to someone else is a big relief. Try simply saying, "I'm so angry (or sad or worried) about my parents getting divorced! It really upsets me!" When the person who's listening can say something back to you like, "No wonder you feel that way, I really understand why you do," it can help you feel even better. Sometimes that's all the talking someone needs to do.

Sometimes it's just the beginning of many more talks you'll have. Talk to a parent. Or if that doesn't feel right, find someone else you really like to talk to, maybe your older brother or sister, your rabbi, a teacher, school counselor, neighbor, or grandparent. It's tough to let it out, but it can really help.

If you have a friend whose parents are divorcing, try to be a good listener when your friend wants to talk. Divorce is never easy.

Sometimes the feelings you have about your parents' divorce are so strong that you may have a hard time concentrating on anything else. When you are very sad, angry, or worried, you may have trouble paying attention in class, focusing on homework, or even remembering what you've just read. If this happens, it's especially important to get some help.

You may feel much better after talking to a therapist, rabbi, counselor, or social worker. These adults are trained to talk with people about their problems and help with feelings that are too intense.

Can you find In this picture a horn, a trowel, a shovel, a saw, a soup ladle, a pitcher, an egg, an artist's brush, a boot, a mug, a telephone receiver, and a kite.

Embarrassment and Divorce

When things change in your family as your parents separate and divorce, it may make you feel embarrassed, bad, or angry. The truth of the matter is a lot of things may change and be different as parents sort out their feelings.

Always remember that you are special and you are no way responsible for your parents' decisions. Don't let careless words spoken in anger or hurt cause you to feel embarrassed or ashamed. You do not deserve to be treated this way.

Our holy books teach us some very important things about embarrassment.

Rabbi Eleazar and the Ugly Man

Our rabbis have taught, "A person should always be gentle as the reed and never unyielding like the cedar."

Once, Rabbi Eleazar son of Rabbi Simeon was coming from the house of his teacher and was riding leisurely on his donkey by the riverside. He was feeling happy because he had studied much Torah.

On the way, he met an exceedingly ugly man who greeted the rabbi, "Shalom Alechem, sir."

The rabbi did not return his greeting but instead said to him, "Boy, are you ugly! Are all your neighbors as ugly as you are?"

The man replied to the rabbi, "I do not know, but go and tell the Craftsman who made me, 'You have made one really ugly vessel!'"

When Rabbi Eleazar realized that he had done wrong, he got off his donkey, bowed before the man, and said to him, "I beg you, forgive me."

The man replied, "I will not forgive you until you go to the Craftsman who made me and say, 'You have made one really ugly vessel!'"

Rabbi Eleazar walked behind him until they reached the man's native city. When his neighbors came out to meet the rabbi, they greeted him with the words, "Peace be upon you, our teacher and our rabbi."

The ugly man asked them, "Whom are you addressing this way?"

They replied, "The man who is walking behind you."

Then he said, "If this man is a teacher, let there not be more like him in Israel!"

The people then asked him, "Why?"

The man responded, "Such and such a thing has he done to me . . . ," and he told them the entire story.

They said to him, "Nevertheless, forgive him, for he is a man greatly learned in the Torah."

The man replied, "Because you asked, I will forgive him, but only on the condition that he does not act in the same manner in the future."

Soon after this, Rabbi Eleazar son of Rabbi Simeon entered the bet midrash (school house) and taught, "A person should always be gentle as the reed and never be unyielding like the cedar. This is why the reed is privileged to be made into a pen for the writing of the Torah, Tefillin, and Mezuzot." (Taanis 20a-b)

What did Rabbi Eleazar do wrong? _____

_____

How could a person who has studied so much Torah do this kind of harm?

_____

_____

_____

When the ugly man said to Rabbi Eleazar, "Go and tell the Craftsman who made me 'You have made one really ugly vessel!'" who is the Craftsman he is talking about? _____

_____

_____

In Genesis 1:27 it says "G-d created people in G-d's image." How could someone who is very ugly be considered to be in G-d's image?

_____

_____

_____

Can someone be pretty or handsome and still be ugly? _____

_____

_____

_____

In the midrash, we are told, "Every time you embarrass another person, you make G-d less. Every time you make another person feel smaller, you make G-d smaller in the world, because people are created in G-d's image" (Genesis Rabbah 24.7).

Explain this midrash in your own words. _____

_____

_____

_____

This story begins with the saying *A person should always be gentle as the reed and never unyielding like the cedar.* What do you think this saying means? _____

_____

_____

What do you see as this saying's connection to the story of Rabbi Eleazar and the ugly man? _____

_____

_____

_____

In the Talmud, we are taught by an unnamed rabbi that "anyone who shames another person in public is like a person who sheds blood." Rav Nahman bar Yitzhak explained this statement by saying, "When people are publicly shamed, their face turns first red (in a blush), then white." The Tosefos, medieval commentators, made this clearer by saying, "when blood drains and the person becomes pale—this is when the blood is shed" (Bava Metzia 58b-59a).

How would you explain "Anyone who shames another person in public is like a person who sheds blood" in your own words? _____

_____

_____

_____

_____

_____

The Boy in the Tower

Once upon a time, a child was born. As he grew older, he felt the anger and heard the war cries around him; he realized he was in the middle of a terrible war. He was in a land with many knights fighting with long swords and lances, archers that showered the countryside with sharp arrows, and people all around him trying to kill and hurt each other. He had no way to defend himself because he was too small to know how to use a sword and he really didn't feel like hurting anyone in any way. But there he was in the middle of a war, and he was forced to do something; otherwise, he understood that he would have been attacked by a knight with sword or lance or by a sharp arrow and killed.

So he built a tower all around himself, hoping that no one would notice that he was there. He felt that if he were not seen, no one could hurt him with one of their weapons. He used trees to build his tower and put no windows or doors in the walls of the tower and covered it with a dark thick roof. He sat within the hiding place, trying to be very quiet, hoping that he had found a way to be safe. He stayed in his tower a very long time. He didn't see the seasons change or the sun set; he never even saw the moon and stars. Time passed and with each day, the boy grew more lonely. He really didn't know what to do about his loneliness; all he knew was that he was very afraid of the war.

One day a little gnome dug down under the safety of the tower and began to run around inside, exploring. The boy became interested in the gnome and asked, "How did you get in here? I thought that no one could get inside my strong tower that has no windows or doors."

"Don't be silly," said the gnome. "There's always a way in, and there's always way out. Just when you think you've built thick walls, you find that they aren't thick at all! Aren't you kind of lonely in here? It's dark and depressing and scary!"

"Yes," replied the boy, "it's pretty bad in here, but I don't know what else to do because I'm in the middle of a war and there's no other place to go."

"Of course there's a place to go," exclaimed the gnome. "Wars aren't everywhere. There's just a battle going on in this place. If we can get you out of here, you can be in a place where there are no wars. It would be nice to live somewhere else. You could walk through the fields and smell the wonderful flowers, run with the deer, watch the frogs play in a pond. Why you could even sing and dance or maybe swim with the fish."

So the boy and the gnome sat down to think of a way to get the boy out from behind the walls of the tower and away from the war. They thought of many different plans. At first they thought that he could build a long tunnel, but that seemed like a tremendous amount of work, and they were afraid that the tunnel might collapse while he was inside it. Then they thought about what would happen if he came out from the wall and ran as fast as he could, hoping that none of the spears or lances would hit him. That idea didn't seem like a good one either.

Then the gnome observed, "Do you realize that when people hold up a white flag during a battle, no one is supposed to hurt them because that is a sign of peace? And it says that you are not dangerous and that you won't hurt anybody. Then you can walk through the war unharmed."

So the boy found a piece of white cloth and tied it to a long stick. He put the gnome in his pocket and, more than a little afraid, came out from the safety of the tower he had built around himself and began to wave the white flag. He walked quicker and quicker, with the gnome telling him how to get away from the battlefield. The people fighting the war saw him and tried to get him to join in the war, but he refused. Each side wanted him to fight for them in battle and be their warrior, but the boy was tired of war and tired of fighting and tired of being angry and scared. He was tired of having walls built all around him, too, and being alone and sad.

The boy just kept walking until he walked away from the battlefield and came to a place where there was no fighting. There were no swords, no lances, no fighting. He found people to take care of him, and he found out what fun and love were all about. He learned many things about himself and his world with these people, but the most special thing he learned was how to stay out of wars so that you don't have to build a tower around yourself. He learned it was all right to be angry, but when anger begins to control you, you're in a war.

Because of all that he had learned, the world became a place for him where he often forgot that wars even existed, and that was the best world of all.

Can You Finish the Picture?

Anger and embarrassment is a terrible thing. It seems that sometimes parents can stay angry at one another forever, but this is not so. It is written in the book of Isaiah that *"when you see the naked, that you cover him, and that you hide not yourself from your own flesh . . . Then you shall call, and the Lord will answer; you shall cry, and He will say: 'Here I am'"* (Isaiah 58:7 and 9).

From this verse in the Prophets we learn of the story of

Rabbi Yose and His Wife

"That you hide not yourself from your own flesh." These words apply to the divorced wife of Rabbi Yose the Galilean from whom he did not hide.

Rabbi Yose the Galilean had a mean wife who used to put him down and embarrass him in front of his students. When his students said to him, "Master, divorce this woman, for she does not treat you with proper respect," he replied, "The marriage settlement I would have to pay her is more than I can afford, so I cannot divorce her"

One time, he and Rabbi Eleazar ben Azariah were sitting and studying, and when they finished, Rabbi Yose asked Rabbi Eleazar, "Will the master come with me to my house?" Rabbi Eleazar said, "Yes." As they entered, Rabbi Yose's wife lowered her face, rudely ignoring the guest. When Rabbi Yose noticed a pot standing on the stove and asked her, "Is there anything cooking in the pot?" she replied, "There is only hash in it." Upon uncovering the pot, however, he found it full of plump chicks. Rabbi Eleazar ben Azariah was in this way made aware that Rabbi Yose's wife was not at peace with her husband.

So as they sat together eating, he observed, "Master, did she not say it was hash? Yet we found chicks in the pot."

Rabbi Yose said, "The chicks are here because of a miracle."

When they finished eating and drinking, Rabbi Eleazar said to Rabbi Yose, "Master, divorce this woman, for she does not treat you with proper respect."

Rabbi Yose replied, "The marriage settlement I would have to pay is more than I can afford, so I cannot divorce her"

Rabbi Eleazar answered, "I will give her the marriage settlement due her." So Rabbi Yose divorced her and was soon married to another woman who was respectful and kind.

The divorced wife's mean ways brought it about that she married the town watchman, a man below her station. After some time, the watchman suffered many problems and sickness. Because of his troubles, he lost his job and soon became blind.

His wife had to hold him by the hand and lead him around all the neighborhoods of the town to beg for alms. When she reached Rabbi Yose the Galilean's neighborhood, she stopped and turned back. Since her husband was very familiar with all sections of the town, he said to her, "Why don't you lead me to Rabbi Yose the Galilean's neighborhood? He, I heard, gives much to charity."

She replied, "I am his divorced wife, and I cannot bring myself to face him."

Once, after making the rounds of the entire town and being given nothing, they reached the neighborhood of Rabbi Yose the Galilean, and again she stopped. When her husband realized why she stopped, he began to beat her, and the noise they made drew the attention of many in the marketplace. Just then, Rabbi Yose happened to look out and, seeing them exposed to public shame in this way, asked the husband, "Why are you beating her?"

He replied, "Because every day she causes me the loss of money from this neighborhood." Upon hearing this, Rabbi Yose took them and settled them in a house he owned and provided for all their needs for the rest of their lives.

The voice of the poor woman was heard at night to say, "It was easier for me to bear the blows of my husband than the pain to accept the charity of Rabbi Yose. The first only injured my body, but the latter touched my very soul within me." (Y. Ketubos 11:3, 34b; Genesis Rabbah 17:3; Leviticus Rabbah 34:14)

Rabbi Yose's Wife's Kitchen Puzzle

Rabbi Yose's wife cooked a lot of food in her kitchen. Can you figure out the anagrams and find the food words?

An anagram is a type of wordplay where the letters of a word are rearranged to make a new word. All the letters in the word are used only once. Can you figure out the anagrams below?

ape   _____

agrees   _____

last   _____

west   _____

cause   _____

fires   _____

keel   _____

team   _____

stakes   _____

soil   _____

Children Can't Fix Divorce!

Just like the divorce is not your fault, getting parents back together is not up to you either. And most likely, this doesn't happen, although plenty of children wish for it and even try things they think might work. Acting like an angel at home all the time (who can do that?) and being perfect at school (another hard thing to do) may make your mother and father happy with you, but it doesn't mean they'll get back together.

The opposite is also true. Getting in trouble so your mother and father will have to get together to talk about these problems is not going to make the divorce go away either. So just be yourself and try to talk to your parents about any feelings you have.

The Two Wives of Ishmael

Ishmael was a hunter and lived in the wilderness for many a day. He and his mother went to the land of Egypt where his mother, Hagar, took a wife in Egypt for her son; and her name was Meriba. Ishmael and his wife had four sons and two daughters. Soon after that, Ishmael set out with his mother, his wife and children, and all his belongings and returned to the wilderness. They made themselves tents in the wilderness and lived in them and used to travel and camp a lot. Hashem gave Ishmael flocks and herds and tents because his father was Avraham. Ishmael and his family lived in deserts and in tents, traveling and resting for a long time. He did not see his father for a long time.

Now the day came when Avraham said to Sarah his wife, "I shall travel to see my son Ishmael, for I wish to see him very much since I have not seen him for a very long time." Sarah was worried that something terrible would happen to Avraham, so she had him promise her that he would not get down from his camel at the place where Ishmael was living. So he rode on one of his camels into the wilderness to look for his son Ishmael. He had heard that he was living in tents out in the wilderness together with all that was his.

Traveling through the wilderness, Avraham at length reached Ishmael's tent at noon. He asked for Ishmael and found Ishmael's wife seated in the tent with her children. Avraham asked the woman, "Where is Ishmael?"

And she said, "He has gone into the field hunting."

Now Avraham was still riding on the camel and had not gotten down from it, for he had promised Sarah his wife that he would not get down from the camel or set his foot on the ground. He asked Ishmael's wife, "My daughter, can you give me a little water that I may drink, for I am tired from my journey"

Ishmael's wife answered Avraham, "We have neither water nor bread." She sat there in the tent and did not look at Avraham and did not ask him who he was. All she did was beat her children in the tent and said many mean and unkind things to them. She than cursed her husband Ishmael and said many hurtful things about him.

When Avraham heard what Ishmael's wife was saying to her children, he grew very angry and displeased that she spoke in such a way. And Avraham called to the woman to come out to him from the tent, and the woman came and stood opposite him, for Avraham was still mounted upon the camel. He said to her, "When your husband Ishmael returns here, this is what you should tell him: A very old man with a long beard came here from the land of the Philistines to seek you and this and that was his appearance, but I did not ask who he was. When he saw that you were not here, this is what he said to me: When your husband Ishmael returns, tell him that this is what that man said: Upon your return, remove the tent peg upon which you have set up this tent and put some other tent peg in its place." Therewith Avraham made an end of his words to the woman and turned the camel about and went off on the camel homeward.

When Ishmael returned in due course from his hunting with his mother and came to his tent, his wife told him: "A very old man came here to seek you from the land of the Philistines, and this and that is what he looked like, but I did not ask who he was. He saw that you were not here and he told me to give you a message: When your husband comes back, tell him this is what the old man said: Remove the tent peg you have here and replace it with another." Ishmael heard his wife's words and understood that it was his father whom his wife had not honored. Also

—

he understood the meaning of what his father had said, and Ishmael divorced her. Then his mother sent for a woman from her father's house in the land of Egypt and brought her to Ishmael's tent in place of the one who had been there.

Three years later Avraham said again, "I shall go once more and see my son Ishmael, for I have not seen him this many a day." So he rode on his camel into the desert and reached the tent of Ishmael at the midday hour. He found Ishmael's wife and asked her, "Where is Ishmael?" The woman came out of the tent and said, "He is not here, good sir, for he has gone into the desert to hunt and herd the camels." And the woman said to Avraham, "Come into the tent, good sir, and eat bread here, for you must be weary to the soul from your journey."

But Avraham answered, "I cannot get down, for I must be quickly on my way. But I pray you, give me a little water to drink because I am thirsty." Then the woman hurried into the tent and brought water and bread out to Avraham and placed it before him and requested him to eat. He ate and drank and felt better at heart and then blessed Ishmael his son.

After eating, he blessed the L-rd and said to Ishmael's wife, "This is what you should tell Ishmael when he returns: A very old man with a long beard came here from the land of the Philistines, looking like this and that, and he said to me: When Ishmael comes here, tell him that this is what the old man said: The tent peg you have placed here in the tent is very good, do not remove it from the tent." Avraham made an end of his words and went riding back to the land of the Philistines.

Ishmael came to his tent, and his wife came out happily and cheerfully to meet him and told him, "A certain old man with a long beard came here from the land of the Philistines and he asked about you, but he has gone away. I brought bread and water out to him, and he ate and drank at his ease, and this is what he said to me: When your husband Ishmael returns here, tell him: Your tent peg is very good indeed, do not remove it from the tent.'"

Then Ishmael knew that it had been his father and that his wife had shown him proper honor, and Ishmael blessed the L-rd.

That was the time when Ishmael rose and took his wife and his children and his cattle and all his belongings and set out from there and went to his father in the land of the Philistines. And Avraham told his son Ishmael exactly what the first wife he had taken had done. And Ishmael and his children dwelt in the land together with Avraham for a long time. (Pirke de-Rabbi Eliezer 30; Sefer haYashar, vaYera 41a-b)

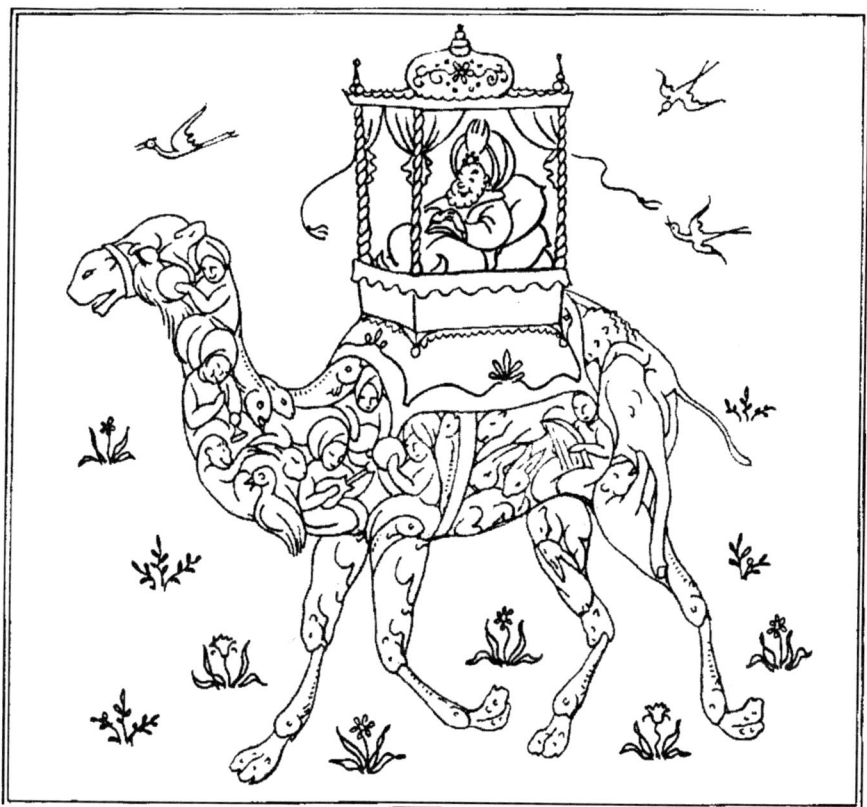

Ishmael learned from his father, Abraham, the importance of welcoming and helping travelers. He would look after all their needs. How many animals, musicians, birds, and fish can you find in the picture?

Derech Eretz—דֶּרֶךְ אֶרֶץ—Is Treating Someone Else with Respect

Sometimes when people go through separation and divorce, they do mean things to one another. They become so angry that they forget that the Torah teaches us to be kind to each other and to always have Derech eretz.

It is easy to be nice to someone you like. It makes sense to do good things for people who take care of you. Derech eretz is doing nice things for others even if you do not know them or like them very much. It is doing good things for others even when they have done nothing for you. *Derech eretz* means doing whatever it takes to make others feel respected.

Derech Eretz, Rain, and the Divorced Couple

In the days of Rabbi Tanhuma, Israel had need of rain, so they came to him and said, "Master, tell everyone to fast (you can't eat or drink during a fast)." He called for a fast for one day, for a second day, and for a third day, yet no rain came down. Then he entered the synagogue and spoke to them, saying, "My children, be filled with kindness for one another, and the Holy One will be filled with compassion for you." Consequently, as they were distributing charity to the poor, they saw a man talking with his divorced wife and even giving her money. At that, they went to Rabbi Tanhuma and cried out, "While we sit here, something very wrong is taking place out there!"

Rabbi Tanhuma said, "What have you seen?"

"We saw this man talking with his divorced wife, and he even gave her money." He sent for the couple, who were brought before the community, and he asked the man, "What is this woman to you?"

The man answered, "She is my divorced wife."

Rabbi Tanhuma said, "Why did you give her money?"

The man replied, "Master, I saw her in great distress and was filled with concern for her."

At this, Rabbi Tanhuma turned his face to Him above and exclaimed, "Master of all universes! When this man—upon whom this woman has no claim for care—saw her in trouble, he was filled with concern for her. Now since it is written of You that You are gracious and compassionate and since we are children of Your beloved ones, children of Avraham, Yitzchok, and Yaakov, and so have a claim upon You for our care, surely, surely You should be filled with kindness for us!" Immediately rain began to come down, and the world enjoyed relief. (Gen. R. 33:3; Lev. R. 34:14.)

Kavōd—כָּבוֹד—Honor

Kavod means honor. It is a very special mitzvah to honor your parents. It is a mitzvah to treat every person with honor and respect. And it is a mitzvah to treat yourself with honor and respect too.

To honor someone, we must work hard. To honor someone, we must be willing to bend like the reed.

Rabbi Simeon ben Yohai said, "Great is the duty of honoring one's father and mother, since the Holy One set the honor due them above the honor due to Himself. For concerning the honor due to the Holy One, it is written, 'Honor the Lord with your possessions' (Mishlei 3:9). How is one to honor G-d with one's substance? One sets aside gleanings, forgotten sheaves, and the corners of the field; [one gives] heave offerings, the first tithe, the second tithe, the poor man's tithe, and the priest's share of the dough; one makes a lulav, a sukkah, a shofar, tefillin, and ritual fringes; one feeds the hungry, gives drink to the thirsty, and clothes the naked. In short, if you have substance, you are obligated to do all these things; but if you have no substance, you are not obligated to do even one of them. When it comes to honoring father and mother, however, whether you have substance or not, what does Torah say? 'Honor your father and thy mother,' even if you have to go about begging in doorways." (Pesikta Rabbati 23/24:2; Mekilta, Yitro, Ba-hodesh, 8)

Sometimes parents get so angry and say things that are mean. They often do things that don't seem fair, it can be confusing and very hard to honor and respect parents. It is very important to remember that you are special to your parents.

Take some time and write down a few things you respect your mother for: _____

_____

_____

_____

_____

_____

Now take some time and write down a few things you respect your father for: _____

_____

_____

_____

When Rabbi Eliezer was asked, "How far should honoring one's father and mother extend?" he replied, "Go and see what a certain man named Dama ben Netinah did for his father in Ashkelon. Once, the sages wanted to buy some precious stones from him for the ephod and were ready to pay him of sixty thousand gold denars. But the key to where the stones were kept was under his sleeping father's pillow, and he would not disturb him." The following year, however, the Holy One gave him his reward. A red heifer was born to him in his herd. When the sages of Israel visited him intending to buy it, he said to them, "I know about you. Even if I were to ask all the money in the world, you would pay me. But all I ask of you is the amount I lost because I honored my father." (Kiddushin 31a)

With everything going on, you may feel a little rejected. The feeling that one has been abandoned by the two closest people in the world hurts a whole lot. You probably have a lot of questions and are trying to understand why these two people whom you love so much cannot stay together and may even blame yourself because you feel that you are not good enough to bring them back together.

It's not you job.
You have no control over what they do.

No matter how angry your parents get over the separation and divorce, they love you. They know that you are special but don't always tell you so. Concentrate on why you are so special to your parents.

Your job is to be the best you there is.

Honor Your Father and Mother

How I Am Like My Parents?

Do people ever look at your mother or father and say you look just like one of them? That you have your father's eyes? Or your mother's smile?

How do you feel about that?

_____

_____

_____

_____

_____

_____

There are probably certain ways that you also look like your mother or father. You may have the same-color eyes. Or your hair may be the same color his or hers was at your age. (Hair color usually changes as we get older! Maybe you can find a picture of your mother or father at a young age and notice ways in which you might appear similar. You might like some of the ways in which you look the same, and you may not like some of them!)

_____

_____

_____

_____

57

Ways I Look like My Loved One:

_____

_____

_____

_____

_____

Perhaps even more importantly, there may be ways that you act like your mother or father or special talents you may have gotten from them. For example, do you laugh like one of your parents? Are you a good artist like your mother or father? Do you find math really easy at school like your mother or father always did? Are you interested in sports like your mother or father? Do you have a fantastic memory like your parents?

Ways I Act like My Parents:

_____

_____

_____

So far, we've looked at features and talents you inherited from your mother and father, like having brown eyes or being good at drawing. You can't really choose the ways that you look like someone or even the special talents you inherit from them. But there are other ways you can choose to be like someone you admire or love. For example, you can be generous and give money to tzedakah as you know your parents do. You can read many books just as he or she does. You can be a loyal friend. It's a very special compliment to choose to be like someone.

A Way I Choose to Be like My Parents:

No matter what they say or do, your parents will always love you. You are very special to them and to everyone in your family.

The rabbis taught, "There are three partners in the creation of man—the Holy One, blessed be He, the father, and the mother. When a person honors his father and his mother, the Holy One, blessed be He, says, 'I consider it as though I lived among them, and they had honored Me.' It was taught, 'It is revealed and known to Him who created the world that a son honors his mother more than his father because she persuades him with gentle words; for that reason the Holy One, blessed be He, placed the honor of the father before that of the mother in the verse, "Honor your father and your mother" (Exodus 20:12). It is revealed and known to Him who created the world that a son respects his father more than his mother because he teaches him Torah; therefore, the Holy One, blessed be He, placed the respect of the mother before that of the father in the verse, "Every person must respect his mother and his father" (Leviticus 19:3). A Tanna recited a baraita before R. Nachman: when a person causes anguish to his father and his mother, the Holy One, blessed be He, says, "It was proper that I did not dwell among them, for if I dwelled among them, I would be distressed to see a child treat his parents this way.'" (Kiddushin 30b-31a)

Can you solve the code?

All About Tongues: Tender Ones and Tough Ones

It can be really hard dealing with divorce, but try to remember that lots of children go through what you're going through, and usually everything and everyone turns out fine. In fact—as bad as things might seem right now—you just might be surprised at how good the future turns out to be!

When people are hurting, they say things they don't really mean. They forget how powerful words can be. We can learn from the rabbis of long ago about how important it is to watch how we express ourselves.

Rabbi Shimon ben Gamaliel said to his slave Tabi, "Go to the market and buy me a good piece of meat." So Taby went out and bought him a tongue.

Later, Rabbi Shimon said to Taby, "Go out and buy me a bad piece of meat at the market." Tabi went out and again bought him a tongue.

Rabbi Shimon ben Gamaliel asked him, "Why, when I asked you to buy me a good piece of meat, did you buy a tongue, and when I asked you to buy a bad piece of meat, did you again buy me a tongue?" Tabi replied, "Because from the tongue comes good, and from it comes also evil. When it is good, nothing is better than it; and when it is bad, nothing is more evil than it." (Leviticus Rabbah 33:1)

It is so true that when someone says something nice to you, you feel special. The words are important, and how they are said makes you feel good. As Tabi said, "When it is good, nothing is better than it."

What are some of the things your mother says that makes you feel special:

What are some of the things your father says that makes you feel special:

Rabbi Yehuda haNasi made a special dinner for his students, serving them tongues that were tender as well as tongues that were tough. The

---

disciples selected the tender tongues and passed up the tough ones. So he said to them, "Pay attention to what you are doing—even as you select the tender and pass up the tough, so let your tongues be tender and not tough toward one another." (Lev. R. 33:1; Yalkut, Tehillim, #767)

Does anyone know how to make a tender tongue? Well, when it comes to making a tongue that won't talk back, you need to do some preparing to make a tender tongue like Rabbi Yehuda haNasi.

Tender Tongue

3-4 pound beef tongue
boiling water
2 onions
1 teaspoon pepper

2 tablespoons vinegar
6 whole cloves
3 cloves of garlic

Wash the tongue in cold water.

You don't want any bad or harsh words on it

1. Place the tongue in a deep pot and cover with water. Turn on the heat to boil the water.
2. Peel and slice the onions and peel the cloves of garlic. Add the onions, garlic, vinegar, cloves and pepper to the water.

Man, is some of this stuff stinky! How can something that smells this bad taste good?

3. Bring the water to a rapid boil then reduce heat and simmer (that's when there are small slow bubbles in the water) for 3-4 hours.

This is a good time to talk and share your feelings.

4. Test to see if the tongue is done by sticking a fork in it. If the fork goes in easily than it is done. Let it stand in the water you cooked it in until it is cool.

Not done talking? Talk some more.

5. Remove the tongue from the water and peel off to rough, tough skin. Slice it thin and eat.

Bet it tastes better than the kind you buy at the deli.

—

Breinigsville, PA USA
14 September 2009
224062BV00004B/67/P